FIRST EDITION

Edited By: **Kelly Hanton**

Designed By: **Anthony Brown** and **Natalie Lindsey**

Acknowledgments

Writing this book has been a journey, and I wouldn't have reached the finish line without the support of many incredible people.

First and foremost, my deepest gratitude goes to my **[partner Sophia Ava]**, who provided unwavering encouragement, endless cups of coffee, and sanity checks throughout the writing process. Their love and patience were invaluable.

My sincere thanks to my **editor, [Kelly Hanton]**, for your keen eye, insightful suggestions, and guidance in shaping this book. Your expertise made a world of difference.

I am also grateful to my agents, for believing in this project and helping me navigate the publishing world. Your support and professionalism were instrumental.

Many thanks to my **friends and colleagues** who offered feedback on early drafts, shared their knowledge, and celebrated the milestones with me. Your enthusiasm and support kept me motivated.

A special thank you to **[anyone who provided specific help, e.g., research assistance, illustrations, blurbs]**. Your contribution is greatly appreciated.

Finally, thank you to the **readers**. This book exists for you. I hope you find it informative, inspiring, or simply enjoyable.

CONTENT

How to use this book

The first section of the book is a layout map. This map depicts the natural features of the land, including mountains, valleys, trails, and bodies of water. By studying the map, you can plan your route, estimate the distance and elevation gain, and anticipate any challenging terrain.

By using a compass together with this guide, you can determine locations and navigate through unfamiliar terrain. This is especially important if you veer off course or encounter unexpected obstacles.

The section on hiking covers crucial aspects of a hiking trail

Including:

- **Trailhead location**
- **Description**
- **Difficulty**
- **Day Hike/Multi Day Hike**
- **Dog/Kid Friendly**
- **Type of hike**
- **Elevation change**
- **Length**
- **Estimated time to complete**
- **Features**
- **Allowed uses**
- **Best time to hike**
- **Tips**

It is important to note that some of these parameters may vary depending on several aspects:

Trail Length

A trail length depends on the starting point and end point used when measuring and may vary from one source to another. At times trail lengths can change over time due to erosion, rerouting, or construction.

The way the trail length is measured can vary. Some sources might use a GPS track, which could account for every twist and turn, while others might rely on a ranger's estimate or a historical map, which might be less precise.

Difficulty

The difficulty of a trail is typically determined by a combination of factors, including:

Terrain: How rough or smooth is the path? Is it mostly dirt, rock, roots, or pavement? Are there obstacles like streams, boulders, or steep drop-offs?

Elevation gain: How much climbing is involved? A steeper or longer climb will be more difficult.

Distance: How far is the total hike? A longer hike will naturally require more endurance.

Exposure: Are there sections of the trail where you'll be high up and at risk of a fall, with no railing or protection?

Trailhead location

Trailhead location might be moved due to many reasons some common factors are:

Safety: This is a big one. If the area around the old trailhead becomes unsafe due to things like erosion, flooding, or danger from falling rocks, park services might have to reroute the trail to a new starting point.

Conservation: Sometimes, a trailhead needs to be moved to protect the environment. If the old trailhead was disturbing wildlife habitat or a sensitive ecosystem, park rangers might create a new trailhead in a less disruptive location.

Estimated time to complete

There are many reasons why estimates for hiking trail completion times can vary so much, even for the same trail. Most common reasons are:

Hiker ability: This is a big one. An experienced hiker with good fitness will move much faster than someone new to hiking or who is out of shape.

Trail conditions: Mud, snow, rocks, and overgrown trails can all slow you down considerably. Weather can also play a big role - rain, wind, and extreme heat can all make a hike more difficult.

Pace: Are you stopping often to take breaks or pictures? Are you hiking with a group that needs to go slower than you might like? All of this can affect your overall time.

Elevation gain: This is a big one - the more elevation you gain, the longer it will take to complete the hike.

Taking breaks: Factoring in breaks for lunch, taking photos, or just enjoying the view is important. Don't forget to schedule some rest time into your hike.

Every effort has been made by the author and editors to make this guide as accurate as possible. However, many things can change after a guide is published i.e. trails may be rerouted or washed away by nature, roads may be closed and many other possibilities. WE HOPE ALL THE USERS UNDERSTAND THIS!!

Introduction

Imagine a world where the sun paints the landscape in hues of pearl and ivory, where silence is broken only by the whisper of wind sculpting endless waves of pure white sand. Welcome to White Sands National Park, a place that defies expectation and invites the soul to wander.

Nestled in the heart of the Chihuahuan Desert, this extraordinary park is a stark contrast to its arid surroundings. Here, gypsum crystals, remnants of a long-gone inland sea, have been transformed by wind and time into a breathtaking expanse of dunes. It's a place where the ordinary becomes extraordinary, where every step is a journey into a surreal, otherworldly realm.

The dunes are not merely a backdrop; they are a living, breathing entity. They shift and change with the wind, creating an ever-evolving canvas of nature's artistry. At sunrise, the dunes are bathed in a golden glow, casting long, dancing shadows. As the day progresses, the white sands take on a blinding brilliance, reflecting the sun's intense heat. And when the sun begins its descent, the dunes are transformed once more, awash in hues of pink and purple.

But White Sands is more than just a visual spectacle. It's a place where the senses are awakened. The crunch of sand beneath your feet, the feel of the cool, powdery grains against your skin, the taste of the desert air—these are experiences that stay with you long after you've left. And then there's the silence. It's a profound silence, broken only by the occasional rustle of wind or the distant call of a desert creature.

As you venture deeper into the park, you'll discover a world teeming with life. Despite the harsh environment, plants and animals have adapted to thrive in this unique ecosystem. Keep your eyes peeled for the elusive desert iguana, the graceful sandhill crane, and the delicate yucca plant.

Whether you're seeking solitude, adventure, or simply a chance to connect with nature, White Sands National Park offers something for everyone. So, pack your sense of wonder and prepare to be captivated by this extraordinary desert oasis.

Geology, History & Wildlife

Geology: A Sea of Sand

White Sands National Park is a geological marvel, home to the world's largest gypsum dune field. This extraordinary landscape is a result of a complex interplay of geological and climatic factors over millions of years.

- **Ancient Seas:** The story begins over 280 million years ago when the Permian Sea covered the region. As the sea receded, layers of gypsum, a mineral composed of calcium sulfate and water, were deposited on the seafloor.

- **Lake Otero:** Millions of years later, a massive lake named Lake Otero formed in the Tularosa Basin. As the lake's water levels fluctuated, gypsum-rich sediments were deposited and recrystallized into selenite, a form of gypsum with large, clear crystals.

- **Wind and Water:** The eventual drying of Lake Otero exposed the selenite crystals to the elements. Strong winds broke the crystals into smaller pieces, creating the fine-grained gypsum sand that characterizes the park. Water played a crucial role in shaping the dunes, as moisture content affects the sand's cohesiveness and mobility.

History: Footprints in Time

Human history at White Sands is as captivating as its geology.

- **Paleo-Indian Presence:** Evidence suggests that Paleo-Indians inhabited the area as early as 12,000 years ago. Their footprints, preserved in the soft gypsum mud, offer a unique glimpse into the lives of these ancient people.

- **Apache and Mescalero Apaches:** Later, the area became home to the Apache and Mescalero Apache tribes, who adapted to the harsh desert environment and developed a deep connection to the land.

- **20th Century and Beyond:** The early 20th century saw increased exploration and settlement in the region. White Sands was designated a national monument in 1933 to protect its unique features. In 2019, it achieved national park status, solidifying its importance as a protected area.

Wildlife: Adaptation in a White World

Despite the seemingly harsh environment, White Sands supports a diverse array of wildlife that have evolved remarkable adaptations to survive in this unique ecosystem.

- **Specialized Invertebrates:** The park is home to a high number of endemic species, particularly invertebrates like moths, which have developed white coloration as camouflage.

- **Reptiles and Amphibians:** Creatures such as the desert iguana and spadefoot toad have adapted to the arid conditions, finding ways to conserve water and regulate their body temperature.

- **Mammals:** While large mammals are less common, species like the white-nosed kangaroo rat and coyote have found niches in the dune field.

- **Birds:** The park is a migratory bird hotspot, with species like the sandhill crane and greater sage-grouse visiting during specific seasons.

White Sands National Park is a living laboratory, constantly evolving and offering new insights into the complex interplay of geology, history, and biology. Its pristine beauty and scientific significance make it a treasured resource for generations to come.

How to Prepare

Before You Go

White Sands National Park is a unique and unforgettable destination. To ensure a smooth and enjoyable trip, careful planning is essential.

Research and Planning:

- **Best Time to Visit:** While the park is open year-round, the best time to visit is during the cooler months, from October to April. Summers can be extremely hot.

- **Park Fees and Permits:** Check the park's official website for current entrance fees and any required permits for specific activities.

- **Accommodation:** While there's no lodging within the park, there are various options in nearby towns like Alamogordo and Las Cruces. Book early, especially during peak seasons.

- **Packing List:** Make a comprehensive packing list based on the time of year you're visiting. Essentials include sunscreen, sunglasses, a hat, water, snacks, comfortable shoes, and appropriate clothing.

- **Check Weather Conditions:** Be aware of the weather forecast. Wind can significantly impact visibility and dune conditions.

Location and Getting There

White Sands National Park is located in southern New Mexico, USA.

By Air:

- The nearest airports are in El Paso, Texas, and Albuquerque, New Mexico.
- From these airports, you can rent a car to drive to the park.

By Car:

- The park is accessible by car via US Highway 70.
- Driving is the most convenient way to explore the park and surrounding areas.

What to Pack

- **Sun Protection:** Sunscreen, sunglasses, and a wide-brimmed hat are essential due to the intense sunlight reflecting off the white sand.
- **Clothing:** Comfortable, lightweight clothing for warm weather. Layers are recommended for cooler months.
- **Footwear:** Sturdy, closed-toe shoes for hiking. Sandals or flip-flops are suitable for camp or relaxing.

- **Water and Snacks:** Pack plenty of water, as there are limited water sources within the park. Non-perishable snacks are also recommended.

- **Camera:** Capture the stunning beauty of the white sands with a camera.

- **Dune Sled:** While you can rent one at the park, bringing your own can save money.

- **First-Aid Kit:** A basic first-aid kit is always a good idea for any outdoor adventure.

Things to Do

White Sands National Park offers a variety of activities for visitors of all ages:

- **Dune Sledding:** This is a classic and thrilling way to experience the dunes.

- **Hiking:** Explore the various trails that wind through the dunes, offering breathtaking views.

- **Photography:** The unique landscape provides endless opportunities for stunning photographs.

- **Stargazing:** With minimal light pollution, the park offers exceptional stargazing experiences.

- **Nature Observation:** Keep an eye out for wildlife, such as desert animals and birds.

- **Picnicking:** Enjoy a meal amidst the stunning white sands.

- **Guided Tours:** Join a ranger-led program to learn more about the park's geology, history, and ecology.

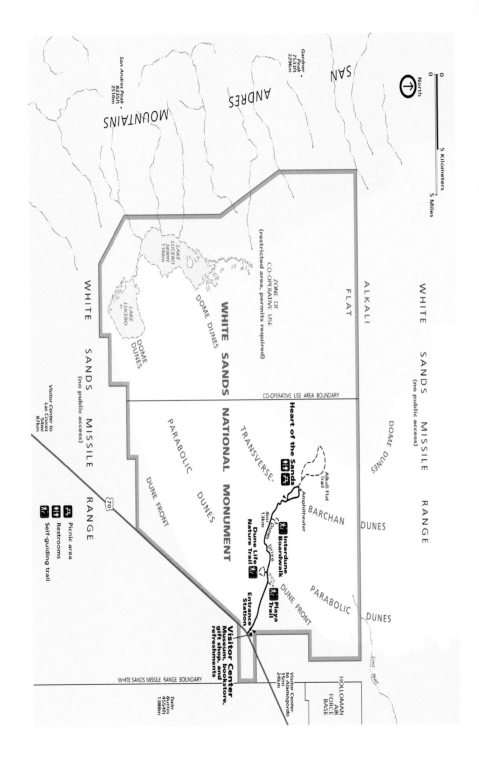

WHITE SANDS MISSILE RANGE

WHITE SANDS MISSILE RANGE
(no public access)

North

0   5 Kilometers
0   5 Miles

SAN

ANDRES

MOUNTAINS

SAN ANDRES MOUNTAINS

Gardner
Peak
7533ft
2296m

San Andres Peak
8235ft
2510m

LAKE
LUCERO
3890ft
1186m

LAKE
LUCERO

DOME
DUNES

DOME DUNES

ZONE OF
CO-OPERATIVE USE
(restricted area, permits required)

WHITE SANDS NATIONAL MONUMENT

ALKALI
FLAT

DOME DUNES

CO-OPERATIVE USE AREA BOUNDARY

Heart of the Sands

Alkali Flat
Trail

TRANSVERSE

PARABOLIC
DUNES

Amphitheater

BARCHAN
DUNES

DUNE FRONT

WHITE SANDS MISSILE RANGE
(no public access)

8mi
13km
Dunes Drive

Interdune
Boardwalk

Dune Life
Nature Trail

PARABOLIC
DUNES

DUNE FRONT

Playa
Trail

Visitor Center to
Las Cruces
54mi
87km

70

Entrance
Station

Visitor Center
Museum, bookstore,
gift shop, and
refreshments

Visitor Center
to Alamogordo
15mi
24km

WHITE SANDS MISSILE RANGE BOUNDARY

HOLLOMAN
AIR
FORCE
BASE

Lost River

Twin
Buttes
4554ft
1388m

Picnic area
Restrooms
Self-guiding trail

Hiking

Easy Hikes

Trailhead

Located within the park, easily accessible from the main park road.

Description

A scenic loop trail that winds through the edge of the gypsum sand dune field. Offers a unique opportunity to observe the transition between desert scrubland and the expansive dunes. Along the trail, informative signs introduce visitors to the diverse wildlife inhabiting the area.

Difficulty

Easy to Moderate. While the trail itself is short, walking on soft sand and climbing dunes can be challenging.

Type of Hike

Loop

Elevation Change

Moderate elevation gain as you climb the dunes.

Dogs are welcomed but must be leashed.

The trail is very family-friendly/ kid friendly with informative signs and opportunities for exploration.

Length

1 mile (1.6 km)

Estimated Time to Complete

Approximately 1 hour

Accessibility

Not ADA accessible. The trail involves climbing dunes and walking on soft sand.

Equipment Needed

Sturdy footwear, water, sunscreen, hat, sunglasses.

Ability

Moderate fitness level required due to walking on sand and climbing dunes.

Features

Scenic, wildlife viewing, educational, family-friendly.

Allowed Uses

Hiking

Trail Surface

Soft sand

Best Time to Hike

Spring (March-May) and fall (October-November) offer pleasant temperatures. Avoid summer heat.

- **Stay on the Trail:** To protect the fragile ecosystem, it's essential to stay on designated trails.
- **Be Aware of Your Surroundings:** Watch for wildlife and avoid disturbing them.
- **Wildlife:** Keep an eye out for the park's unique wildlife, such as white mice, lizards, and various bird species.
- **Photography:** The surreal landscape provides incredible photo opportunities. Bring your camera and experiment with different angles and perspectives.
- **Sledding:** While not part of the trail, many visitors enjoy sledding down the dunes. Bring a sled for some extra fun.
- **Explore Beyond:** The Dune Life Nature Trail is just the beginning. After completing the trail, venture out and explore the vast dune field.

Views from Dune Life Nature Trail

Interdune Boardwalk Trail

Trailhead

Located along the main road, Dune Drive, in White Sands National Park. It's about 4.5 miles from the fee station. There's a decent-sized parking area at the trailhead.

Description

The Interdune Boardwalk is an elevated walkway that traverses the fragile interdune area, offering a unique perspective of the vast white sand dunes and the surrounding landscape. Informative panels along the boardwalk provide insights into the park's geology, wildlife, and ecology.

Difficulty

Easy

Type of Hike

Out and back

Elevation Change

Minimal

Dogs are not allowed

The trail is Kid Friendly

Length

0.4 miles (0.6 km) round trip

Estimated Time to Complete

Approximately 20 minutes

Accessibility

Fully accessible for wheelchairs and strollers.

Equipment Needed

None, except for comfortable walking shoes.

Ability

Suitable for all ages and fitness levels.

Features

Scenic views of the dunes, informative panels, accessible for all.

Allowed Uses

Hiking, photography, nature observation.

Trail Surface

Boardwalk

Best Time to Hike

The park is open year-round, and the boardwalk is enjoyable in any season. However, mornings and evenings offer cooler temperatures, making them ideal for hiking.

Tips

- **Unique Ecosystem:** Learn about the fascinating plants and animals that thrive in this unique environment.
- **Stunning Views:** Enjoy panoramic views of the endless white dunes.
- **Easy Walk:** The boardwalk is a short and easy walk, perfect for all ages and fitness levels.
- **Educational Experience:** Informative signs along the trail provide insights into the park's geology and ecology.
- **Explore Beyond:** While the boardwalk is a great starting point, don't hesitate to venture off onto the dunes for a more adventurous experience.
- **Consider a Sunset or Sunrise:** The changing light creates magical colors in the dunes.
- **Pack a Picnic:** Enjoy a meal amidst the stunning scenery.
- **Check for Park Updates:** Visit the White Sands National Park website for the latest information on closures, fees, and special events.

Views of Interdune Boardwalk Trail

Playa Trail

Trailhead

The Playa Trailhead is located on Dunes Drive, about 2.7 miles from the visitor center. It's a small parking area on the side of the road.

Description

The Playa Trail is a short, easy hike that explores a playa, a dry lakebed that fills with water during rain storms. It offers a unique opportunity to learn about the changing ecosystem of the area. Along the trail, there are interpretive panels that explain the playa's importance and the creatures that inhabit it.

Difficulty

Easy

Type of Hike

Out and back

Elevation Change

Minimal

Dogs are welcomed but must be on a leash.

The trail is short, easy, and informative suitable for kids

Length

0.5 miles (0.8 km) round trip

Estimated Time to Complete

30 minutes

Accessibility

The trail is accessible to most people.

Equipment Needed

Sturdy shoes, water, sunscreen, and a hat.

Ability

Suitable for all ages and fitness levels.

Features

Educational, scenic, kids and families

Allowed Uses

Hiking, walking, nature observation

Trail Surface

Sand

Best Time to Hike

The Playa Trail can be hiked year-round. However, the playa is most interesting after rainfall when it's filled with water or growing crystals.

Tips

- **Stay on the trail:** Protecting the delicate ecosystem is essential.
- **Explore the playa:** At the end of the trail, you can venture onto the dry lake bed. Be cautious of the terrain.
- **Observe wildlife:** Keep an eye out for interesting plants and animals that thrive in this unique environment.
- **Take your time:** Enjoy the peaceful atmosphere and soak in the scenery.
- **Visit during the cooler months:** Spring and fall offer pleasant hiking temperatures.
- **Combine with other trails:** The Playa Trail can be easily combined with other hikes in the park.
- **Respect other visitors:** Share the trail and be mindful of others.

Views from Playa Trail

Lake Lucero Path

Note: The Lake Lucero Path is not a typical hike. It's a guided tour that requires special access due to its location within a restricted area.

Location

The Lake Lucero Path is located within White Sands National Park, but it's in a restricted area accessible only through guided tours. The trailhead is on the White Sands Missile Range property, about 25 miles southwest of the park.

Description

The Lake Lucero tour is a unique opportunity to visit a remote part of the park. You'll traverse rough desert terrain and washes to reach Lake Lucero, a fascinating geological feature. The tour is focused on learning about the lake, its history, and the surrounding environment.

Difficulty

Moderate. The terrain is uneven and requires a moderate level of fitness.

Type of Hike

Out and back.

Elevation Change

Moderate elevation change as you descend to the lake and then ascend back to the trailhead.

Dogs are not allowed on the tour.

Not recommended for young children due to the rough terrain, heat, and remote location.

Length

Approximately 1.5 miles round trip.

Estimated Time to Complete

About 1-2 hours, including the guided tour.

Accessibility

Not accessible. The tour requires special permission and is not suitable for people with mobility issues.

Equipment Needed

Sturdy hiking shoes, sunscreen, hat, water, and camera.

Ability

Moderate fitness level required.

Features

Unique geological features, desert landscape, and the opportunity to learn about the area's history.

Allowed Uses

Hiking only.

Trail Surface

Rough desert terrain with washes.

Best Time to Hike

Cooler months (November to March) are generally more pleasant.

Tips

- **Guided Tour Only:** Unlike other areas of the park, Lake Lucero is accessible only through a guided tour.
- **Limited Availability:** Tours are offered monthly from November to April and require reservations well in advance.
- **Rough Terrain:** The trail is challenging and involves steep gullies. Wear sturdy shoes.
- **Geological Insights:** Learn about the formation of the White Sands dunes and the role Lake Lucero played.
- **Selenite Crystals:** See stunning exposed selenite crystals, crucial to the dune formation.
- **Unique Landscape:** Experience a different side of the park with vegetation and terrain unlike the main dune field.
- **Book Early:** Reservations fill up quickly, so plan ahead.

Moderate Hikes

Alkali Flat Trail

Trailhead

Located in the northwest section of Dunes Road, right after you make the turn around the loop.

Description

The Alkali Flat Trail offers a unique experience through the heart of the White Sands National Park. It winds through towering dunes, offering breathtaking views of the endless white sands. The trail gets its name from the Alkali Flat, a dry lakebed at the end of the trail.

Difficulty

Moderate to Challenging. While the trail is not exceptionally long, the constant ascent and descent of sand dunes makes it physically demanding.

Type of Hike

Loop.

Elevation Change

Significant elevation changes due to climbing and descending sand dunes.

Dogs are not allowed on the trail.

Not recommended for young children due to the challenging terrain and potential for getting lost. Older children with good hiking experience may enjoy the adventure.

Length

Approximately 5 miles (8 km).

Estimated Time to Complete

3-4 hours, depending on your pace and physical condition.

Accessibility

Not accessible. The trail is not ADA compliant.

Equipment Needed

- Sturdy hiking shoes
- Plenty of water
- Sunscreen
- Hat
- Sunglasses
- Map or GPS device

Ability

Good physical condition and experience hiking in sand is recommended.

Features

- Scenic views of the white sand dunes
- Opportunity to explore a unique desert ecosystem

Allowed Uses

Hiking only.

Trail Surface

Soft sand.

Best Time to Hike

Early morning or late afternoon to avoid the hottest part of the day. Spring and fall offer pleasant temperatures for hiking.

Tips

- **Stay on the marked trail:** The sand can be disorienting, and it's easy to get lost.
- **Pace yourself:** Hiking in sand is more tiring than you might expect. Take breaks as needed.
- **Protect yourself from the sun:** Reapply sunscreen regularly, wear a hat, and seek shade when possible.
- **Watch for wildlife:** Keep a respectful distance from animals and avoid disturbing their habitat.
- **Carry a map:** Even with the marked trail, a map can be helpful.
- **Consider hiking barefoot:** Many people find it surprisingly comfortable and refreshing to hike barefoot in the cool sand.
- **Bring a camera:** The stunning scenery is worth capturing.
- **Early morning or late afternoon:** These times offer cooler temperatures and better lighting for photography.
- **Hydrate before, during, and after:** Proper hydration is crucial for preventing heat-related illnesses.

Views from Alkali Flats

Trailhead

The trailhead for the backcountry trail is located about 6.5 miles from the visitor center, along Dunes Drive. It's the second-to-last trailhead before the park boundary.

Description

The Backcountry Camping Loop Trail offers a unique opportunity to immerse yourself in the surreal white sand dunes. It's a relatively short loop that provides a taste of the backcountry experience without demanding too much physical exertion.

Difficulty

Moderately challenging. While the trail itself is relatively short, walking on soft sand can be physically demanding.

Type of Hike

Loop

Elevation Change

Minimal elevation change. The trail is mostly flat, following the contours of the dunes.

No, dogs are not allowed on the trail

Older children who are physically fit can enjoy this hike. However, young children may find the sand challenging.

Length

Approximately 1.7 miles

Estimated Time to Complete

Around 29 minutes, but this can vary depending on your pace and stops.

Accessibility

The trail is not accessible for people with disabilities.

Equipment Needed

- Sturdy hiking shoes
- Sunscreen
- Hat
- Water
- Backcountry camping permit (if camping overnight)

Ability

Intermediate hiking ability is recommended.

Features

- Scenic white sand dunes
- Opportunity for backcountry camping

Allowed Uses

Hiking and camping.

Trail Surface

Soft white sand.

Best Time to Hike

The park can be very hot in the summer, so early morning or late afternoon is ideal. Spring and fall offer pleasant hiking conditions.

Water Conservation: While there are no water sources in the backcountry, proper hydration is crucial. Bring enough water for your entire trip.

Sun Protection: The desert sun is intense. Protect yourself with sunscreen, a hat, and sunglasses.

Wildlife: Keep a respectful distance from wildlife. Avoid feeding animals and store food properly to prevent attracting them.

Sand Navigation: Walking on sand can be challenging. Take your time and adjust your pace accordingly.

Night Sky: Enjoy the incredible stargazing opportunities. The lack of light pollution makes for an unforgettable experience.

Backcountry Camping

- **Campsite Selection:** Choose a campsite that is at least 100 feet from the trail and any water sources.

- **Fire Restrictions:** Check for fire restrictions before your trip. Campfires might be prohibited during certain times of the year.

- **Food Storage:** Properly store food and scented items to avoid attracting wildlife.

- **Toilet Facilities:** There are no restrooms in the backcountry. Pack out all human waste.

Camping

Note: Backcountry camping in White Sands National Park is currently closed due to rehabilitation of camping sites. There is no confirmed reopening date yet.

General Information

- **Type:** Backcountry camping
- **Number of sites:** Not specified, as sites are dispersed along the backcountry camping loop.

Campground Features

- **Amenities:** None. Backcountry camping is primitive.
- **Toilets:** Vault toilet located approximately one mile from each campsite.
- **Showers:** None.
- **Water:** Not available. You must carry in all water you need.
- **Other:** No electric hookups, RVs, or trailers allowed. Camping is restricted to tents.

Operation Seasons

- Typically open year-round, but currently closed.

Fees

- Backcountry camping permit required. Fees may apply. Check the park's official website for the most current information.

Accessibility

- **Wheelchair access:** Not accessible.

- **RV and trailer access:** Not allowed.

- **Campground classification:** Primitive.

Reservations

- Reservations are not available for backcountry camping. Sites are first-come, first-served.

Important Considerations

- **Permits:** Obtain a backcountry camping permit before setting out.

- **Water:** Carry enough water for drinking, cooking, and hygiene.

- **Waste:** Pack out all trash and human waste.

- **Weather:** Be prepared for extreme temperatures and wind.

- **Wildlife:** Encounter wildlife, such as snakes and coyotes.

- **Safety:** Carry a first-aid kit and emergency supplies.

Basic Information

- **Location:** Oliver Lee Memorial State Park, New Mexico, USA

- **Distance to White Sands National Park:** Approximately 30 minutes

- **Number of Sites:** 44

- **Electric Hookups:** Yes, available

- **RVs:** Allowed

- **Tents:** Allowed

- **Walk-in:** Not applicable

- **Group Sites:** Available

- **Horse Camping:** Not allowed

Campground Features

- **Amenities:** Electric hookups, showers, restrooms, dump stations, group shelters, visitor center, historic ranch house, nature trails

- **Toilet Type:** Flush toilets

- **Shower Type:** Standard showers

- **Water Facilities:** Potable water available

Operation Seasons

- Year-round, however, peak season is October through April.

Fees

- Fees vary depending on the type of site and time of year. It's best to check the New Mexico State Parks website for the most current pricing information.

Accessibility Information

- The park and campground are generally accessible to people with disabilities, including wheelchair users. However, specific accessibility details for individual campsites and facilities should be confirmed with the park directly.

- RVs and trailers are accommodated, but site sizes may vary.

- Campground classification: Developed

Reservations

- Reservations are recommended, especially during peak season. You can make reservations through the New Mexico State Parks reservation website or by calling their reservation line.

Note: While Oliver Lee Memorial State Park is a great base for exploring White Sands National Park, it's important to remember that the two parks are separate entities with different fees and regulations.

Additional Tips:

- The campground can be windy, so consider bringing appropriate gear.

- Pack plenty of water, as the desert climate can be dry.

- Be prepared for changing weather conditions, as desert temperatures can fluctuate significantly between day and night.

Alamogordo / White Sands KOA Journey

Location

The Alamogordo / White Sands KOA Journey is located in Alamogordo, New Mexico, not within White Sands National Park itself. It's a convenient basecamp for exploring the park, situated about 15 miles away.

Basic Information

- **Number of sites:** The campground offers a variety of sites to accommodate different camping styles. It has sites for RVs, tents, and cabins. Exact numbers can vary, so it's best to check their website for the most current information.

- **Electric hookups:** Available for RV sites.

- **RVs:** Accommodated with various site types and electric hookups.

- **Tents:** Designated tent sites available.

- **Walk-in:** No specific information found about walk-in sites.

- **Group:** The campground has a large rec room and covered patio suitable for group events.

- **Horse:** No horse camping is allowed at this KOA.

Campground Features

- **Amenities:** The campground typically offers amenities such as a pool, rec room, playground, and possibly a camp store.

- **Toilet type:** Flush toilets are standard at KOA campgrounds.

- **Shower type:** Hot showers are usually available.

- **Water facilities:** Drinking water is accessible throughout the campground.

Operation Seasons

The campground is typically open year-round, but weather conditions can affect operations. It's advisable to check their website for specific dates.

Fees

Fees vary depending on the site type, time of year, and any additional amenities used. It's recommended to check the KOA website for the most accurate pricing information.

Accessibility Information

- **Wheelchair access:** While many KOAs strive for accessibility, specific information about wheelchair access at this location should be confirmed by contacting the campground directly.

- **RV and trailer:** The campground accommodates RVs and trailers with various site options.

- **Campground classification:** This KOA is considered a **developed campground** with amenities and facilities.

Reservations

Reservations are highly recommended, especially during peak seasons. You can make reservations through the KOA website or by contacting the campground directly.

Note: It's always a good idea to check the official KOA website for the most up-to-date information on amenities, fees, and availability.

Dog Canyon Dispersed Campground

Location: It is located at 436 Co Rd A16, Alamogordo, NM 88310, USA.

Basic Information

- **Number of Sites:** Unlimited (dispersed camping)
- **Electric Hookups:** None
- **RVs:** Allowed, but sites are not designated and may not be level.
- **Tents:** Allowed
- **Walk-in:** Not applicable (dispersed camping)
- **Group:** Not designated, but multiple groups can camp together.
- **Horse:** Allowed

Campground Features

- **Amenities:** None
- **Toilet Type:** None
- **Shower Type:** None
- **Water Facilities:** None

Operation Seasons

Year-round

Fees

- **Dispersed Camping:** Free

Accessibility Information

- **Wheelchair Access:** Not accessible

- **RV and Trailer:** Accessible, but sites are not designated and may be uneven.

- **Campground Classification:** Primitive

Reservations

- **Reservations:** Not available. This is dispersed camping.

Important Note: Dog Canyon is a dispersed camping area, meaning there are no designated campsites, amenities, or facilities. It offers a truly wild camping experience with stunning scenery. Be prepared for self-sufficiency and pack out all trash.

Additional Information:

- While there are no amenities at Dog Canyon, there is a campground with water and a dump station just outside the entrance.

- Be aware of wildlife and practice Leave No Trace principles.

Location

Aguirre Spring Campground is situated on the east side of the Organ Mountains, approximately 21 miles east of Las Cruces in Dona Ana County, New Mexico. It is approximately 40-50 miles to White Sands National Park depending on the route.

Basic Information

- **Number of sites:** 55 individual campsites and 2 group campsites.
- **Electric hookups:** None.
- **RVs:** Allowed, but sites are not designed for large RVs.
- **Tents:** Allowed and suitable for camping.
- **Walk-in:** Not applicable.
- **Group:** Two group campsites available.
- **Horse:** Not allowed.

Campground Features

- **Amenities:** Picnic tables, fire rings.
- **Toilet type:** Pit toilets.
- **Shower type:** None.
- **Water facilities:** Water is available only at the entrance to the campground by the Camp Host Site area.

Operation Seasons

Open year-round.

Fees

- $7 per campsite per night.

- $50 per group site per night (reservations required).

- $5 per vehicle for day use and $15 per bus.

Accessibility Information

- **Wheelchair access:** Not suitable for wheelchairs due to terrain.

- **RV and trailer:** Allowed, but sites are not designed for large RVs.

- **Campground classification:** Developed (has amenities like picnic tables and fire rings).

Reservations

- Individual campsites are first-come, first-served.

- Group campsites require reservations.

Note: While there is no official mention of wheelchair accessibility, the terrain of the campground, with its location in mountainous terrain, suggests it would be challenging for wheelchair users.

Additional Information:

- The campground offers stunning views of the Organ Mountains and Tularosa Basin.

- There are hiking trails in the area.

- Cell phone reception can be limited.

Glossary

Campground classification - Campgrounds have been classified into two main types: developed and primitive

Developed Campgrounds

Developed campgrounds are those that offer a variety of amenities and facilities to campers. These amenities can vary depending on the specific campground, but they typically include:

- Designated campsites: These are marked areas where campers can pitch their tents, park their RVs, or set up other camping shelters.

- Restrooms: Developed campgrounds will have restrooms with flush toilets and running water. Some campgrounds may also have vault toilets, which are self-contained toilets that do not require plumbing.

- Water: Developed campgrounds will have a source of clean drinking water, such as a well or spigot.

- Picnic tables and fire rings: Most developed campgrounds will have picnic tables and fire rings at each campsite.

- Other amenities: Some developed campgrounds may also offer other amenities, such as showers, laundry facilities, camp stores, playgrounds, and swimming pools.

Primitive Campgrounds

Primitive campgrounds, on the other hand, offer few or no amenities. These campgrounds are typically located in more remote areas and are designed for campers who are looking for a more rustic camping experience. Primitive campgrounds may have some or all of the following:

- Designated campsites: Some primitive campgrounds may have designated campsites, but these are often simply cleared areas of land.
- Fire rings: Primitive campgrounds may have fire rings, but this is not always the case.
- No amenities: Primitive campgrounds typically do not have any other amenities, such as restrooms, water, picnic tables, or trash collection.

Trail difficulty - refers to a rating system that helps hikers choose trails that are appropriate for their fitness level and experience. Here's a breakdown of common trail difficulty categories:

Easy: Easy trails are generally short (less than 2 miles) and have a flat or gentle incline. They are suitable for hikers of all ages and fitness levels, including young children and families.

Moderate: Moderate trails are moderately challenging and may be longer (2 to 4 miles) with some steeper sections and elevation gain. They are suitable for hikers in good physical condition who are comfortable walking for a few hours.

Challenging: Challenging trails are more difficult and may be longer (4+ miles) with significant elevation gain, steep inclines, and uneven terrain. They require good physical fitness and some experience hiking on challenging terrain.

Strenuous: Strenuous trails are the most difficult and are typically long (4+ miles) with significant elevation gain, steep inclines, and difficult terrain. They require excellent physical fitness, strong hiking skills, and experience navigating difficult trails.

Elevation change - This is the overall variation in height you'll experience on the trail. It considers both going up (elevation gain) and going down (elevation loss).

Features- is simply any interesting or noteworthy aspect of the trail itself. This could include things like scenic overlooks, waterfalls, wildflowers, or historical markers.

Loop Hike - is a more intricate and diverse form of hiking. As the name suggests, in a Loop hike, you start and finish at the same trailhead, but you follow a circuitous route that doesn't require retracing your steps. Here are the characteristics that make Loop hikes appealing:

1. **Variety**: Loop hikes offer a rich diversity of scenery, as you traverse different terrains, ecosystems, and vistas. You won't see the same section of the trail twice.

2. **Sense of Accomplishment**: Completing a loop hike often feels more satisfying, as you've circumnavigated a specific area and returned to your starting point without repeating any segments of the trail.

3. **Adventure**: The element of uncertainty and exploration is more prominent in loop hikes, as you might not know exactly what's around each bend. This adds excitement and a spirit of adventure to the experience.

4. **Efficiency**: Loop hikes make efficient use of your time and energy since they don't require doubling back. This

can be especially appealing when you have a limited amount of time for your hike.

However, Loop hikes also have their challenges, such as potentially more complex navigation and the need for good trail markers. Some hikers might find the unpredictability of the terrain and the possibility of getting lost a bit daunting.

Out and Back Hike

The "Out and Back" hike, also known as a "there and back" hike, is one of the simplest and most straightforward hiking formats. In this type of hike, you begin at a designated trailhead and travel along the path until you decide to turn around and return to your starting point. Here are some key features of Out and Back hikes:

1. **Simplicity**: Out and Back hikes are ideal for beginners and those who prefer a straightforward, no-fuss approach. Since you retrace your steps, navigation is often more straightforward, reducing the chances of getting lost.

2. **Predictable Terrain**: Knowing that you'll return on the same trail means you have a good understanding of the terrain. This allows you to plan and pace your hike more accurately.

3. **Scenic Views**: Out and Back hikes often lead you to the same stunning viewpoints on your return journey, offering a different perspective of the landscape you've just traversed.

4. **Flexibility**: You can customize the length of your hike by choosing how far you want to venture from the trailhead, making it suitable for hikers of all levels.

However, there are limitations to Out and Back hikes. The monotony of retracing your steps can become less engaging for some, and the predictability of the terrain might not provide the variety that loop hikes offer.

Overlook - refers to a specific location on a trail that offers a particularly scenic or panoramic view of the surrounding landscape. These are often high points, such as cliffs or mountain summits, that provide unobstructed vistas.

Hikers often aim for overlooks as a reward for their effort on the trail. They can be a great place to take a break, enjoy the scenery, and snap some pictures.

RV Sites - RV sites are designated areas within a campground or RV park specifically designed to accommodate recreational vehicles (RVs) like motorhomes, travel trailers, and fifth-wheel trailers.

Tent Sites - A tent site is a designated area within a campground specifically designed for pitching tents. These sites typically have a cleared, level area of ground suitable for setting up a tent, and may also include amenities like a fire ring, picnic table, and sometimes a lantern post.

Trailhead – refers to the starting point of a trail. It's essentially the place where you leave the road or developed area and begin your trek on the designated path.

Extra Notes

Made in the USA
Middletown, DE
18 December 2024

67647387R00029